GW01157339

An Anglesey Summer
First published 2009

Designed by J. C. Davies

ISBN: 978-1-84524-152-0

Published by:
Llygad Gwalch, Ysgubor Plas, Llwyndyrys, Pwllheli, Gwynedd LL53 6NG

01758 750432
01758 750438
books@carreg-gwalch.com
Internet: www.carreg-gwalch.com

WE THANK - - - - -

- - - - everyone who has given time, interest, and information for this book, and in some cases, permission to photograph. Your co-operation is much appreciated.

In particular, John wishes to place on record his appreciation of the generous help of John Cave, M.B.E., and Richard Burnell for supplying photographs of events which took place in Holyhead at a time when he was busy elsewhere.

We thank Gwasg Carreg Gwalch, too, for welcoming the project and for their expertise and pleasant working relationship while it was in production.

IT WAS EARLY SUMMER

Summertime on Anglesey offers many attractions.

Those of us who are fortunate to live on the island welcome the opportunity to enjoy the company of friends and relations. City dwellers appreciate the spectacular scenery and the peace as they walk the coastal path. Water sports which come into their own as our resorts don their summer dress appeal to many.

Villages organise special events which highlight the island's rich historical past, on land and sea. Children are catered for in many ways.

Local newspapers, Tourist Information Centres, Internet, and community centre notice boards convey information about special activities. There is always something being planned for the summer in Anglesey. We are a sociable community on our island.

Come with us, in pictures and words, as we record a taster of some of the events which took place during 2008 - only some, as it would need a volume twice the size to record them all.

John *(J. C. Davies Photography)*
Margaret *(Margaret Hughes text)*

Beaumaris Festival

Beaumaris Festival is held over one week as May turns into June. It always attracts hundreds of visitors to the old town. They come to listen to classical, popular music, and jazz, according to their preference, or to hear poetry readings or an annual lecture.

Some merely choose to stroll around the town, absorbing the unique atmosphere of the Festival. Art and craft are included in the varied programme through exhibitions and demonstrations and the popular craft fair on The Green. The first Beaumaris Festival was held in 1986. It has become a fixed annual tradition.

A popular feature of the Festival this year was a breathtaking display by the Royal Air Force Red Arrows team, as they swooped over the Menai Strait, creating designs in the sky, applauded by "oohs" and "aahs" from onlookers on the hill and shore of the Menai Strait.

(bottom centre and right) It only took one of the Red Arrows three seconds to leave the party and achieve this height.

The David Hughes Centre in Beaumaris, once the old established grammar school, now completely refurbished for its new role as a community centre, made an excellent venue for the art exhibition. Beaumaris boasts an enthusiastic and talented art group which meets here. Their exhibition was a popular part of the Beaumaris Festival.

The success of the Festival is due to commitment of many residents and supporters who take on individual responsibilities. One of these is David Bower, seen (*below*) as he admired a portrait of the Centre caretaker, Les Chaffer, painted by an art group member.

(*above*) A visitor to the craft marquee on The Green admired the expert workmanship of an Anglesey cabinet-maker.

The Great Menai Strait Raft Race. This unusual race attracted competitors and a crowd of sightseers along the shores of the Menai Strait on a wild and windy day. The race was the culmination of hours of work, of building, and of preparation for the crews, some of whom enter each year. This year a fair number of craft obeyed the starter's order at Felinheli, with Porthaethwy as their goal. Rafts varied in size and shape according to the whim of the competitors. They were made of virtually anything which would float. As well as creating excitement for the crews and enjoyment for the watchers on shore, the race was a money raiser for charities.

(*above*) The winning raft is seen some way ahead of its rivals, dwarfed by the mighty span of the suspension bridge.

(above and left)
The winning raft Groundhog reached Porthaethwy, to the acclaim of onlookers.

John persuaded the crew of the winning raft, nick-named “Groundhog”, to pose with non-sailing parents, Bob and Mary Mason of Llantrisant, on whose land the raft was built, for a victory picture. All agreed the weather had been unhelpful. Several crews braved the elements, but “Groundhog” was the only raft to arrive at Porthaethwy without the aid of Beaumaris Lifeboat which was on hand to give help if needed. The race has been a feature for some years. It is now organised by Porthaethwy residents.

The Anglesey Walking Festival - - - - With the completion of the Anglesey Coastal Path, the 2008 Walking Festival took on new meaning, its popularity was evident as groups met to be conducted on the various sections by knowledgeable leaders.

The Festival was organised by Menter Môn with the National Trust, the Countryside Commission for Wales, Ynys Môn County Council, the Wildlife Trust and the Ramblers Association. The event has become an important one in the summer calendar. As May turned into June, nine charity walks were a splendid opportunity to view countryside and the seashore. John took his camera on the walk from Rhoscolyn headland, guided by Edward Ivor Jones, an expert on the region who told the group of shipwrecks, explained the geology and answered many questions from the walkers.

(above) Edward Ivor Jones can be seen pointing to a small upright stone with the following engraving on it, "Tyger September 17 1819." There are a few stories associated with this small memorial stone, the most familiar is that Tyger, a dog, guided his master and crew to the safety of the shore, when their small ship sank. All the crew on board were saved, but sadly, Tyger died of exhaustion.

(above) Bwa Gwyn (White Arch) once the site of an active china clay industry. Following the quarrying of the cliff face, small boats carried the rock to awaiting larger ships at anchor in the bay.

(left) John Davies Retired Professor of Geology, pointing out the intensely featured strata of the New Harbour Group.

(above) Edward Ivor Jones entertaining the walkers with his many stories of Rhoscolyn. Above Porth Saint the legend has it that Saint Gwenfaen daughter of Pawl Hên of Ynys Manaw (Isle of Man), made her cloister here. Gwenfaen was chased away from her cloister by druids and escaped by climbing the rock stack off Rhoscolyn head. The tide came in and angels carried her away, hence the name Porth Saint.

(right) There is interest at every turn on the coastal path. Edward and John inspect this curious specimen, apparently used in the perfume trade a long time ago.

Making a brief stop at St Gwenfaen's well, Edward told the story about this sixth Century "holy" well with healing powers said to cure mental disorders; it was customary to throw white quartz pebbles into the water. The Anglesey Walking Festival in now an annual event.

Cestyll - A "Hidden" Garden

Late spring and early summer are the months to see gardens at their best. Anglesey has several open to the public at this time of the year. One of these is the so-called "hidden" garden at Cestyll, now owned by the nuclear power station at Wylfa. It is opened to the public on two days in the year, early spring and late summer. Admission fees are given to charities.

Cestyll has an interesting story. There was once a house here, now demolished, which belonged to the Hon. Violet Vivian, one-time lady in waiting to Queen Alexandra. She created the garden in a rocky cleft made by a swift-running stream, in which she grew many of the plants one can see there today.

Now, nearly a century later, it is cared for by staff from Wylfa and volunteers. In her day, Violet Vivian opened the garden to local people to help charity, too, so it is appropriate that the tradition continues.

Visitors can wander along the pathways, appreciating the care which goes into the upkeep of this garden today. The mill at the foot of the cleft is not open to the public. It is owned by the National Trust.

Information about the garden opening may be had from the Visitor Centre at Wylfa.

Cestyll offers beauty, peace and quiet on this north coast of Anglesey. Trees, shrubs, and water combine to make a garden of delight.

Anglesey Vintage Equipment Society Rally - - - - Late May saw imposing steam engines and eye-catching vintage cars en route to Henblas, Llangristiolus, to disport themselves at the annual rally. What memories they evoked among the older visitors who could remember seeing similar vehicles in use during child--hood, while younger visitors marvelled at these gentle giants. The rally was not competitive. Each year it aims to keep members in touch, with the chance to discuss problems.

(above) Observers press themselves alongside the safety fence to admire the gentle and quiet strength of the steam engine, in a demonstration of pulling power.

From the right, Hon Secretary of the Society John Phillips, with fellow founding members Emyr Owen and Derek Griffiths.

The first rally organised by the Society was held at Llangefni marketplace in 1977 with the help of local farmers. Since then it has been held at Plas Coch, Llanedwen, but moved to Henblas five years ago, now its permanent home.

Among this year's exhibits was Aveling and Porter Engineers engine by Royal Letters Patent No.2438, made in Rochester, Kent in 1889, now owned by Neil Williams on a smallholding outside Whitchurch, Shropshire. Known familiarly as "Valentine", it was saved for posterity during the early 1950s before coming into Neil's possession.

These rallies are family affairs. This year Neil brought along his seven years old daughter, Hannah, pictured posing proudly with Dad.

Public bodies exhibit, as well as individual owners. An example was the steam fire engine now owned by Cheshire Fire Service, in the loving care of Billy Cadwallader Davies. This was built by Shand, Mason, & Co, Engineers London about 130 years ago, bought second hand in 1916 by Highfield Tannery, Runcorn, and later given to Runcorn Town Council. Its bright red livery and compact size and shape attracted many interested viewers at this year's rally.

Once a common sight in Holyhead, this Fiat Tipo Zero 1913 HP 10/15 was owned by a local doctor. It was later found in a farm barn and extensively refurbished and arrived at the rally looking smart and elegant.

This Model T Ford was once used as a taxi in Pwllheli. It appeared at the rally with gleaming black bodywork and bright red wheels.

Llanfechell Music Festival - - - The garden at "Brynddu" was once the delight of 18th century squire and diarist, William Bulkeley, who created it. On this occasion, over three hundred years later, it was enjoyed by a gathering who had come to relax and be entertained by some wonderful music. John's camera caught some of the atmosphere as visitors and concert goers enjoyed supper.

This festival was organised by the Mechell Community Group in remembrance of a one-time member who had contributed greatly to the area during his life-time. The generosity of tenor Gwyn Hughes Jones, born on the island, and his wife, soprano Stacey Wheeler, pianist Iwan Llewelyn Jones, Côr Meibion y Traeth (Male Voice Choir) and other local artistes made the evening a resounding success.

This was an outdoor event, held on a summer evening in the beautiful grounds of "Brynddu," Llanfechell. Pictured above are the world-famous operatic singers, Gwyn Hughes Jones and Stacey Wheeler.

Soprano Stacey Wheeler charmed her audience and Côr y Traeth with her voice and personality.

Iwan Llewelyn Jones, described in the "Daily Telegraph as seemingly conjuring a whole orchestra from his instrument", Iwan is now established as one of Britain's most imaginative and successful pianists. He has performed to audiences world wide, and in 2006 made his North American solo recital debut in San Francisco, and will perform in Wigmore Hall's prestigious Sunday Morning Coffee Concert series.

Iwan studied at Oxford University and the Royal College of Music where he won several awards and competitions for both academic and pianistic excellence.

Those who have read William Bulkeley's diary will remember his love of his garden. That tradition prevails today as the care taken by the present owner, Professor Robin Grove-White, is obvious. Lawns are fringed by some of the finest trees on Anglesey.

Gwyn Hughes Jones and Stacey Wheeler have performed on stage world-wide. Gwyn was born at Llanbedrgoch on the island, trained at the Guildhall School of Music and abroad. Stacey is a product of Indiana, Pennsylvania. Following her education at Stetson and Florida University she, too has sung all over the world.

Côr Meibion y Traeth, based at Benllech, are the island's show-stoppers where male voice singing is in question. As well as performing throughout Wales they, too, have appeared on the world's stages.

The extensive grounds at "Brynddu" took on an informal festive look as concert-goers enjoyed their picnic suppers out of doors, on a perfect summer evening.

The concert was such a success that it is hoped this Festival at Llanfechell will have been the first of many such annual events in the village.

St. Cybi's Church, Holyhead Flower Festival - - - Anglesey's programme of summer events would not be complete without several flower festivals, held in the island's churches and chapels, John chose to visit Holyhead's parish church of St. Cybi where an ambitious, beautifully designed display was a focus of attention in the town. Here a band of artistic and nimble fingered ladies had created a superb display both thoughtful and beautiful. In a church which has been the centre of worship for several centuries, it was appropriate that the theme was a commemoration of the contribution of service to Holyhead from St. Cybi himself to the late Lord Cledwyn of Penrhos, sixteen in all, using flowers, text, and illustrations where possible.

The display pictured above commemorated the life of Commander John Macgregor Skinner, R.N.

Today, flowers of all kinds are widely available for most of the year, and full use was made of them, resulting in wonderful splashes of colour and form at every turn. Dark corners were lit by nature's hues.

(above left) Lord Cledwyn of Penrhos, MP for Anglesey from 1951 to 1979. House of Lords 1979 to 2001.
(above right) Trevor Lovett, Headmaster Holyhead Grammar School 1946 to 1950. Comprehensive 1950/64.

It was as though the floral decorations enhanced the already grace of the old building, and made visitors look anew at stained glass designed by Edward Burne-Jones and made in the William Morris workshop and the massive angel of Carrera marble guarding William Owen Stanley's tomb. All making a wonderful backdrop to the festival.

The display pictured above recorded the tireless work for the town of the Hon Oliver Stanley and Lady Kathleen Stanley.

For this occasion, every corner of the church held a commemorative display. There was plenty for the visitor - and visitors came in their droves to see and appreciate the generous spirit existing in the town over the centuries.

The Spanish Lady in Red.

Chapels, too, had their Flower Festivals during the summer. Capel Hên as here, at Llanrhuddlad, where rich colour softened architectural austerity.

Clear glass allowed natural light to fall on exquisite displays of flowers in this nonconformist chapel, where simplicity was the keynote.

Substantial sums are collected for charity at many events held on Anglesey over the summer. These cheerful children made sure that visitors to Capel Hên, Llanrhuddlad, emptied their pockets before leaving.

The parish church at Llanfechell, dating from the 6th century, also held a flower festival, the theme being "The Universe". How local 18th c. diarist, William Bulkeley, would have been pleased to see his own parish church used in this way, as he was a notable gardener at "Brynddu."

Medieval Beaumaris Edward 1'st castle at Beaumaris did not reach its potential, as it was never completed. But it did, nevertheless, see some action during the Glyndwr Revolt of the early 15th century, and was garrisoned briefly during the Civil Wars. Its design has always been ....

Visitors were intrigued to know about foods available, and culinary expertise, of the Middle Ages. Household crafts had to be common knowledge when the real "Milwyr Glyndwr" lived.

.... regarded as the most sophisticated in Europe. This summer a group of medieval period enthusiasts, "Milwyr Glyndwr," brought a touch of authenticity demonstrating various aspects of the way of life in the Middle Ages. Their visit during the summer caused a deal of interest among visitors and residents alike.

(above) A modern day housewife watched with interest as her medieval counterpart showed her skills.

There was no jousting at Beaumaris in 2008, no horses to be seen but other martial arts were demonstrated. Modern day medieval knights fought with weapons of the period, keeping the men and boy visitors enthralled. This was a day when history was brought to life at Beaumaris Castle.

Today's medieval historians, suitably dressed, posed for a 21st century picture in the interior of Beaumaris castle.

Amlwch Viking Festival --- During July Amlwch attracted many to its Viking Festival. They lined one bank of the port where they were reminded colourfully of the Viking raiders who once caused havoc in Anglesey. As dusk fell, excitement mounted as a horde of stalwart "Norsemen" appeared over the brow of the hill, shouting and waving flamed torches. They rushed to the harbour embankment and hurled their flaming torches into the purpose built Viking Ship, which immediately caught fire, to the rapturous applause of the watching crowd.

Holyhead Maritime Festival - - - The weather smiled on the colourful event, held in the New Harbour and along the Newry Beach. The picture above shows Holyhead from the sea across to the Maritime Museum which was the focal point of all the colourful happenings on shore, as shown on the following pages. This event draws a crowd of onlookers and participants every year, rain or shine, and this year was no exception.

HEDDLU ATEGOL
POLICE SUPPORT
Cerys Haf

AMGUEDDFA ARFOROL
MARITIME MUSEUM

Q636 WMJ

IRISH FERRIES

South Stack and Ellin's Tower

Until it opened to the public recently, few had been able to visit the South Stack Lighthouse, operated by Trinity House. This summer scores of hardy walkers took the path down the cliff face and descended the stone steps to the suspension bridge which took them across the narrow channel on to Ynys Lawd. Visiting the lighthouse was an experience they were not likely to forget. Another attraction, too. Ellin's Tower, built by William Owen Stanley as a summer house for his wife, is now one home of the RSPB who welcomes visitors to use their binoculars to watch bird life on the cliffs above the Stack, in crevices and ledges and pictures on live television from cameras attached to the cliff face. The sea cliffs provide habitat and nest sites for around 4,000 birds to use, including Choughs the rarest crow in the UK.

Botanists, too, are welcomed at Ellin's Tower. Here they can see plants and flowers and seabirds including puffin, chough, peregrine, guillemot, razorbill, fulmar and gannets at close quarters through the binoculars, a delight especially in spring and summer.

"Well worth the effort" was the comment of visitors who climbed all those cliff face steps back to Holy Island from South Stack and their time well spent at Ellin's Tower. "Now for a welcome cup of tea".

Lifeboats
47-013

SEA FOOD

Lifeboat Day At Moelfre

- - - - - Anglesey's tradition of life saving at sea from several lifeboat stations around the coast is well known. Moelfre is one. Since 1848 hundreds of lives have been saved by the crews of successive lifeboats. The name of Dic Evans, late coxswain of the Moelfre lifeboat, an intrepid fearless seaman, is almost legendary in RNLI circles.

Usually quiet, the village came to life one day during the summer, with all manner of events to raise money for the RNLI. Supporters flooded in to the car parks early, determined to find a place.

A frequent occurrence in real life, co-operation between the yellow rescue helicopter from RAF Valley and the lifeboat crew demonstrated in the bay.

P
RAF
RESCUE

A cheery wave from bystanders for the excellent display by the local lifeboat and RAF Valley search and rescue helicopter, while the bronze statue of Dic Evans at his wheel kept watch from above the crowd.

Open Day At "Swtan."

At Church Bay, on a fine summer day, visitors made their way down to explore Anglesey's last thatched cottage, "Swtan". This is a remarkable restoration, carried out through the enthusiasm of local residents who did not wish to see the old cottage fall into decay. The restoration has been done to reflect how life was lived here during the early years of the last century when there were still many such cottages on the island.

In those days the occupants were agricultural workers, their needs simple, their lives often reflecting hardship. "Swtan" may be small, but there was much to see inside and outside.

(above) The living room, with curtained off area to the right for cooking.

(left) The ladder to the "croglofft".

(right) Ground floor bedroom.

Outside various country crafts were demonstrated, all of which might have been done by the erstwhile occupants.

The Anglesey County Show--- is the eagerly awaited event in the summer calendar. Here the island's farming community meets, along with others from further afield, on its permanent show ground at Mona. This year, although the summer had been wet, the weatherman smiled kindly

This is one of the largest provincial shows in the country, with a history dating back to 1876. As usual, there was the excitement of competition, and some fine beasts to admire. Crafts, too, had their place as did flowers and food.

(above left) A proud porker showed its paces.

(above right) There was keen competition in the sheep classes.

(left) A young family helper endeavoured to control a frisky exhibit for judging.

(above) Here in the cattle shed, owners saw to the welfare of their beasts.

(left) However, there was time for the family of Bradog Farm to socialise, before judging commenced.

(left)

No mistaking the speciality of Hogia Bryn-Awel Herefords, of course.

(bottom)

Whilst one man shelters beneath the umbrella, four magnificent shire horses are primed, prior to entering the main ring.

(above) "Let us show the judge what you can do".

(left) One gentle giant won a prize for his smiling owner.

The Anglesey Show was not all about animals. Flower arranging classes were popular. Exhibits brought touches of colour and elegance to one corner of the show-ground, where natural beauty predominated.

A mouth watering display of home grown vegetables and food drew the admiration of everyone.

(above left) This convincing witch was a winner in a Scarecrow competition by children.

(above right) Cake dressing connoisseurs discussed the merits of the entry.

(right) Models on the catwalk at the fashion show held in the Young Farmers Marquee.

(top left) Even gentle giants need a few words of comfort.

(top right) "I could be the next world champion, I only need to encourage my parents to buy it."

(*left*) "Would it be missed if Cai drove the big yellow dumper away?"

Winners of their classes, prepared for the Grand Parade.

(above left) There was some--thing so elegant about dressage.

(above right) But nothing so grand as a heavy horse.

(left) "Look at me, I am the prettiest of them all."

This was the sight many had come to see, nothing like show jumping to give pleasure.

(right) Always entertaining to the show goers, "Robinsons brewers' dray".

The 17th Art For All Exhibition - - - - The Ucheldre Centre at Holyhead was the venue for this art show, a yearly event which attracts scores of entries and visitors during August. This year substantial prizes were distributed to adults, young people and children from local schools who had used a variety of media to express their thoughts with pen, pencil and brush. There was a special prize for "Best on Show," chosen by visitors. This exhibition brought more friends to the Ucheldre Centre, those on holiday who may never have visited before. Many voiced their approval of the use being made of the restored buildings and the excellent facilities there.

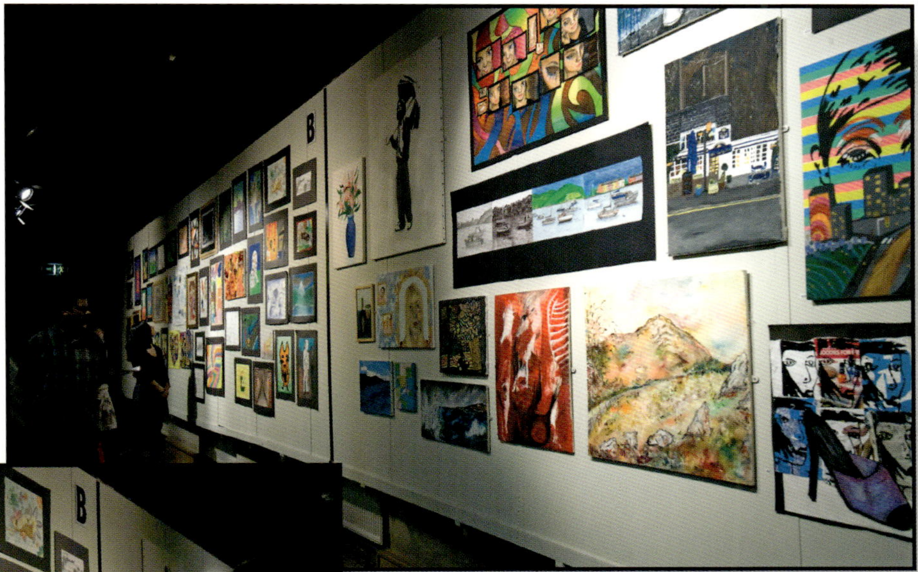

The walls of the gallery at Ucheldre were a riot of colour, admired by those who took part and visitors.

Llynnon Mill --- where the sails really do turn! It is twenty five years since Llynnon Mill, Llanddeusant, then newly restored, welcomed the public. Now it is known as being the only working windmill in Wales. This summer it proved an attraction as popular as ever to local visitors and tourists alike. A new extra attraction was added as a group of replica round houses, superbly thatched and built as they would have been centuries ago, are open for public viewing. Given a fine day, a wind blowing and turning the sails merrily, and the added attraction of round houses, watching grain being ground and turned into flour, a well stocked shop and a popular mill café - what more could a visitor wish to see?

The round houses attracted parties of local school children who could learn how their ancestors experienced communal living centuries ago. And a visit was an eye opener to parents, too.

Watching the miller doing his job fascinated these children who then bought flour in the well stocked shop. And enjoyed tea in the café before leaving.

Summer Sailing

The sea around the Anglesey coast is a magnet for yachtsmen from all over Britain. Sights such as these could be seen throughout the summer when regattas were popular.

It was an arresting sight as Fife One Design yachts lined up for the start of racing from the Gazelle Hotel on the Anglesey shore, pictured against the dark brooding clouds over the Carneddau Mountains.

(above) Menai Strait One Design yachts getting into line for the start of a day's racing.

(left) A Fife One Design yacht in fine form for the afternoon of racing on the Menai Strait.

(*below*) Mr W. H. Rowland M.I.M.E of Deganwy, designed in the late nineteen thirties a classic 20ft sloop for sailing on the Menai Strait. Built of mahogany on oak frame with a lifting centre plate, and specially designed for the exciting waters of the Menai Strait. Built by boat builders Morris & Leavett of Gallows Point Beaumaris.
MS1 "Britannia" built in 1937 and affectionately known as the Marks and Spencer of the Menai Strait.

(*above*) Sailing on the Menai Strait
"Fife One Design Class"

In 1926 plans were sought from top designers in the yachting world, William Fife 111 and R. B. Fife, of Fairlie, for a new class of sailing boat suitable for the waters of the Menai Strait and the Conwy estuary. Fifteen were built by A. M .Dickie & Sons' boatyard at Bangor, at a cost of £275 each. Fourteen of the Fife class are still in existence.

William Fife O.B.E once said that the secret of a great yacht was that it should be both "fast and bonnie."

Village Shows

(right)

Summer village shows abound. Here, at Llaingoch, Holyhead, the crowd who arrived to compete or to support a family member, or merely to browse through the entries and enjoy the atmosphere. The display of home cooking, art and crafts and home grown produce brought out the judge in everyone. Entries were closely considered and judgement made.

(left)

There were competitions for children, too - after all, they are the adult participants of the future.

56
Llaingoch
Summer Show
FLOWERS • CRAFT

1st

Llanddona And Beaumaris Horse And Pony Show

(page 77)

Six years old Catrin Frazer, on her pony, "Peachy" showing the cup - the Robin Roberts Challenge Cup - which she won at the show. This annual show is always well attended, and popular with young riders.

(right) A show jumper of the future - who knows?

(above left) Even ponies need a rest sometimes.

(above) "I feel a great deal more vivacious after that short rest".

(left) Decision time as the judge pondered which prize to give.

(above left) Catrin competed in the ring.

(bottom left) Competitors face the judges.

(top right) A quick gallop before the contest.

(bottom right) Anxious time as they waited to enter the ring.

Carnival Time At Cemaes

This year Cemaes Bay Carnival brought out scores of residents and visitors to the little town, whose streets hummed with activity. Among the attractions were the Coffin Dodgers Skiffle Group who entertained outside. Alf Pritchard excelling on washboard and drum, with fellow members in harmony.
Carnival queens from other towns and villages went along too and created a dash of beauty and colour. Charitable causes benefited from the event.
(carnival collage on page 82)

PRINCESS
ELOISA
Cemaes
Carnival
Amlwch
A5025

Amlwch 5
A5025

WALES AIR AMBULANCE QUEEN

THE
STAG

Amlwch 5
A5025

Picnic With A Porpoise - - - On a tranquil evening a group of wildlife enthusiasts met at Point Lynas, determined to glimpse the shy harbour porpoises who frequent the water there. They were not disappointed, although one had to be quick to catch sight of them. Binoculars and cameras were at the ready all evening.
The evening was organised by the North Wales branch of the Wildlife Trust.

Above harbour porpoise off the north Anglesey coast.

Staff from the Wildlife Trust were on hand to advise and answer questions

Sailing at Treardddur Bay --- Trearddur Bay Sailing Club is one of the busiest on the island, from August 1st to August 31st. There has been a tradition of sailing for pleasure here since the club was founded in 1919, mostly by wealthy holiday makers from Liverpool and the Wirral, whose families had long since had a holiday home at the Bay. Travelling today is very different from then, arriving by train at Holyhead Station, having months before booked your horse and cart to carry the family luggage along a narrow winding country road to the small sea-side hamlet for a month of sailing.

(above) Seabird Half-Raters negotiating the narrow and rocky outlet from Porth Diana into the bay.

(pages 86-87) Preparing to leave Porth Diana for a morning of racing.

GBR
51427
GBR
48342
GBR
51014

(top left) We watched a potential winner of the Vendée Globe, as he sailed at ease in "Gladiator."

(bottom) Half-Raters leaving the bay towards Porth Y Post mark, with Holyhead Mountain for a backdrop.

Myths, so colourful in their red sails and varnished hulls. Myths have been part of Trearddur Bay Sailing Club from its setting up in 1919. It was the club decision at the beginning to have these 14-footers built at Mathew Owen Menai Bridge, and Rowlands Boatyard Bangor.

(above) Half Raters approached a marker buoy in the Bay. Snowdonia, in the background, looked regal.

(left) Class 420 Dinghy two person trapeze and spinnaker racing dingy, in fine form.

(above) Class 420 Dinghies off to a cracking start.
(right) Class 420 powered down to win.
(bottom) Half Raters on a bearing towards Porth Y Post mark.

(left) Shadowed by two Half Raters and sailed proudly by a youngster under the age of 16. in "Oppymistic" the optimist is the most popular single-crew sailing pram in the world, designed by the American Clark Mills in 1947 for children up to the age of 15.

(below) Seabird Half Rater Scoter, crossing the winning line. Half Raters were introduced to the Club in 1922. No 6 Scoter was built in 1898/9 by R. Latham & Co Crossens.

The New Kyffin Williams Gallery at Oriel Ynys Môn

Oriel Ynys Môn, Llangefni, always a honey-pot of artistic talent as well as presenting the history of Anglesey to adults and children in separate galleries, drew thousands of visitors during the summer to see enhancing new developments, including a spacious gallery to display the Oriel's large, valuable collection of work by Anglesey and national artist, Kyffin Williams.

Art lovers came from all over the world, to admire, and to pay homage to the Anglesey artist who created a genre all his own.

The gallery has been designed for visitors to stand back for a good view of the large paintings, or to have easy access for close up reading of accompanying descriptive text.

Last minute visitors took advantage of spaciousness then visited the well stocked shop and patronised the tempting café.

Old Gaffers At Holyhead - - no,

not a derogatory term for the elderly, but an affectionate name given to gaff-rigged ships. Members of an Association hold races annually. In addition, it is becoming an annual event in Holyhead at the end of August, and there were plenty of people around, to enjoy these magnificent boats on display.

Races were first run in the Solent in 1956. Boats are not necessarily old, members all over the world are building boats from various kinds of materials, however, they must be gaff-rigged to qualify.

Gaffers in the grand parade of sail, sailing past The Holyhead Maritime Museum, escorted by the Holyhead Lifeboat, "Christopher Peace." This gave diners at the Museum Bistro a close-up view.

(above left) Some of these boats carry plaques on board which tell their history to the visitor. The converted St. Davids Lifeboat covered 84000 nautical miles between 1984–1993, on its circumnavig--ation of the World. It is also dedicated to the memory of Ieuan Bateman of Treginnis who was lost overboard on the 8th November 1956, when this Lifeboat "Sŵn Y Môr" was returning from the rescue of eight men of the French Trawler "Notre Dame De Fatima."

(top right) This diminutive steam driven launch moved silently, surrounded by much larger boats.

(above) "Naomh Crónán" sailed past in the Grand Display of Sail.

(above right) Stories to be told of long-ago - - sailing adventures.

At this event, brightly dressed uniformed soldiers of the 7th Hussars, closely associated with the action at Waterloo when Henry Paget, 1st Marquess of Anglesey was so prominent, boarded "Vilma" to fire a gun from its deck in celebration of the day.

Anglesey Racing Circuit at Tŷ Croes --- The track at Tŷ Croes was popular during the summer when the Lancashire and Cheshire Car Club celebrated its 85th birthday with a programme of motor sprint. The Tŷ Croes race track, commonly known as the Anglesey Circuit, claims to be the most exciting and significant development in British motor racing in recent years. Anybody interested in motor sport is welcome, whether driver or onlooker. On this day as drivers took to the track, cameras were at the ready to capture their driving capabilities. There is every feature to test the motorist, sharp bends, cambers, undulations, and breathtaking scenery, unrivalled for a racing circuit.

621
38

Speed and careful driving in wet and dry conditions went hand in hand and, yes, they did occasionally break down --- that's what it was all about.

Steam Threshing Day - - - this was one of the more unusual events. On September 13th whole families went in their droves to the Anglesey Steam Threshing Day at Llechog, Bull Bay. Preparations had been made several weeks previously with corn harvested using a binder, and stooked for three weeks according to the old tradition, then carried to the harvest field with due ceremony. The 101-years old threshing box in use was operated in the early 1940s by now octogenarian Richard Williams, pictured right.

Onlookers could appreciate an old method long since disbanded, and see how well the old machine did its job.

(main picture and top right) Other country crafts were demonstrated, too. Not many visitors had ever seen a sculpture like this by Roz, made entirely from ivy.

(left) In the children's section others showed their skills with vegetables.

Philip demonstrated countryside materials and tools for a number of purposes, and showed many of his skills.

Holyhead Breakwater Model Boat Club - - - Summer Sundays and Wednesdays found members of this club meeting at the Holyhead Breakwater Country Park. Boats come in all shapes and sizes. Members derive as much pleasure from sailing their models, as do the yachtsmen from their actual-size craft. *(bottom)* "Perkasa class" Gas Turbine Torpedo Boat at full speed ahead. Commissioned in 1967 for the Malaysian Navy.

(top page) Air sea rescue and target-towing launch "Halifax" was ready for action on the lake.

(right) Off for the afternoon sail.

(top) Through the age spectrum, with hi-tech radio control transmitters.

(right) "Smaragd" sailed elegantly, controlled by her master.

(left)

The fishing and racing Schooner "Bluenose" was built in Nova Scotia and launched at Lunenburg in March 1921 to fish in the rough waters off the coast of Newfoundland. During the prohibition era, she was used as a rum runner. She was lost off Haiti in 1946.

(right)

Fire-fighting boat "Düsseldorf". The vessel is designed specifically to cope with disaster situations in the ports of the Ruhr industrial region of Germany.

The Anglesey Woodland Festival

From the sea to the woodlands. This festival was held at Carreglwyd, Llanfaethlu.
The green grounds were the right venue for a number of activities, all concerning Anglesey's woodlands. Visitors were pleasantly surprised at the use made of natural material for a number of crafts.

Ingenuity in the use of materials easily available was a feature of this Woodland show, greatly appreciated by visitors who returned home inspired.

One of the demonstrators who drew attention was Jo Alexander, working on her springpole lathe. It all looked so easy, but was it?

Jo worked in miniature, too. She made a baby's rattle with a dexterity marvellous to see.

He's done it all before! Fire lighting was made easy the Boy Scout way by two sticks and some friction.

Instant success! But a little expertise helps.

(above) Five years old Emma tried her hand, helped by mother, to create a handbag from paper and scraps of fabric.

(right) Painting paper cows was quite difficult.

There was no end to the variety of objects carved from wood. Meticulous work went in to carving flowers, watched by a fascinated young onlooker who was delighted to be presented with the finished flower.

You never knew what you might come across in the woods! Duncan Kiton's interpretation in wood of the immediately recognizable iconic sculpture by Auguste Rodin, "The Thinker".

(below)
Duncan carving his sculpture with a chain saw.

Dafydd Cadwaladr, a tree surgeon and woodland expert from Bethesda demonstrated his flair and skill in sculpturing a chair, from a tree trunk, into a sought-after children's chair. All done in two minutes and thirteen seconds.

It was a Festival with a difference, hugely successful in promoting nature's materials.

The Anglesey Marathon - - - During September hundreds of would be marathon runners, families and friends, made their way to the Anglesey Agricultural Show ground at Mona. There was a festive feel everywhere with stands and stalls to please everyone. This event was organised by Menter Môn, with an army of friends and volunteers.

(left and above) It only took three seconds for the front-runners to cover the above distance, as captured in the four photographs above, at the begin of the half marathon. An hour, eighteen minutes and four seconds later the winner was crossing the finishing line.

For some the anxiety started to accumulate, for others it was time to have a chat before they started on the ten-kilometre race, and then, heads down and they were off.

Gary Norgrove from Wrexham, winning the half marathon in one hour and eighteen minute and four seconds, congratulated Holyhead Olympic marathon runner Tracey Morris, on achieving second place, in one hour eighteen minute and fifty-one seconds.

There were rules which had to be obeyed in the enthusiastic Dragon's dash, a five kilometre race for juniors.

asics
536
asics
652

Royal Air Force Valley. Freedom of Anglesey Celebrations

Another annual summer event took place in Llangefni in September when Anglesey County Council re-affirmed their appreciation of the long-standing occupation by the RAF of the Valley station. This was a re-enactment of the presentation of the Freedom of the island to the RAF.

(above) Band of the Royal Air Force playing during the main ceremony outside the County Hall.

(left) Displaying the Freedom Charter outside Llangefni Town Hall, during the march past.

Scenes from the Freedom Ceremony in front of the County Hall.
(above left)
Chair of the Council Councillor Aled Morris Jones inspecting the guard of honour.
(below)
Band of the Royal Air Force leading the parade past the Chairman Councillor Aled Morris Jones, Lord Lieutenant Huw Morgan Daniel, and Valley Station Commander Group Captain Neil Connell.

(above) Royal Air Force Band marched to the left, followed by RAF personnel from Valley, past the Bull Hotel, admired by an onlooker for their outstanding music and style.

The End of summer ----- we hope you have enjoyed this brief record of some of the events which took place on our island during 2008. Many will be repeated in years to come. Why not take YOUR camera out and about, and record for yourself some of your favourite activities?

John C. Davies (photographer)
Margaret Hughes (text)